SCRUNCHED PHOTOS OF THE WORLD'S GREATEST WORKS OF ART

HAND-SCRUNCHED
BY CARL REINER

RANDOM CONTENT INK LLC
Beverly Hills, CA 90210

www.RandomContent.com

**RANDOM
CONTENT**
PUBLISHING

Published 2019
FIRST EDITION

Published by RANDOM CONTENT INK LLC
ISBN: *978-0-9995182-5-0*

Library of Congress Control Number:2019918841

Book Design by: Carl Reiner
Photography by Lawrence O'Flahavan
Dust Jacket by: Aaron Davis – aarondavis.com

Any people depicted in images have given approval by their estate and trustees.

This book is printed on acid-free paper.

Printed and bound in India by Replika Press Pvt. Ltd.

SCRUNCHED PHOTOS OF THE WORLD'S GREATEST WORKS OF ART

HAND-SCRUNCHED
BY CARL REINER

"Nobody squishes or scrunches art like Carl Reiner, my aged buddy. (I'm not far behind) Carl continues to create in unususal ways that stimulate and intrigue. He has selected the most wonderful and most scrunchable art of all time."

- Steve Martin

"Scrunched Photos of Celebrities, Hand Scrunched by Carl Reiner" was such an unbounded success that I decided to personally scrunch the artwork of the World's Greatest Artists."

- Carl Reiner

"In 'The Dick Van Dyke Show,' Mary Tyler Moore as Laura Petrie had posed for a painting."

"I played artist Serge Carpetner who painted her portrait and titled it, 'October Eve.'"

"At a prestigious high-end art gallery, Laura shocked upon viewing the nude portrait of herself for which she had posed wearing a sweater, slacks and a scarf, which Carpetner chose not to include. As Pablo Picasso often said, 'Art is the elimination of the unnecessary.'"

- Carl Reiner

FOREWORD

How do we look at art today? What is art? Is there a connection that we are missing in our busy lives?

In this book Carl Reiner has created his own masterpiece. While allowing the reader to interact with each page we are able to quiz ourselves and/or learn about the artist, their art and their place in the art history timeline. In this book we see the trend that movements take only to become replaced with another movement.

As a Fine Arts and Art history teacher I find that most students enter the classroom thinking that art is all about having fun without direction.

I remind my students that art is created to serve as a reminder of the innate human urge to give expression to the eternal problems of existence.

(stated by Lawrence S. Cunningham and John J. Reich)

Artists are not individuals who mindlessly throw paint on a canvas. They have direction, tried methods, rules of design to follow or break, a personal challenge that needs to be fulfilled, and a story that needs to be told. Visual art has a purpose and a voice. It is a lasting impression on our timeline of life. This is history, and it matters.

I am happy to state that my students realize that making art is not an absent minded process but one that has purpose and is everlasting.

Creating art requires direction and knowledge of how to use mediums in order to achieve the desired effect. Art that makes history, is the process of an individual who has chosen to use this knowledge to represent social issues. Artists represented in this book have showcased the courage with their process. They change the way the mediums were intended to be used, therefore creating a new idea for other artists to follow.

"Art is not what we see but what we make others see."

(Edgar Degas)

I am humbled when my students come to the realization of their success as well as what it takes to create the "World's Greatest Works of Art".

While reading this book I learned new things about the "scrunched" artworks, and even more interesting, I enjoyed the opportunity to learn about new pieces that I have not seen. In turn, this allowed me to learn a bit about Carl and the places that he has seen, as well as the collections that he holds dear. Art has the beautiful way of allowing us to see the humanity and culture of others.

Carl's creative method made it possible to make learning fun again, whether it is in a tangible book form or with a device. As a teacher, I look forward to incorporating this book in my classroom as a learning tool.

I know you will have fun with this interactive masterpiece!

Chelon Perez-Benitoa

Master of Arts in Arts Education (MAAE)

National Board Certified

AP Fine Arts and Art History teacher

SCRUNCHED PHOTOS OF THE WORLD'S GREATEST WORKS OF ART

HAND-SCRUNCHED BY CARL REINER

MONA LISA
LEONARDO DA VINCI

Leonardo da Vinci's The Mona Lisa has been described as the best known, the most visited, the most written about, the most sung about, and the most parodied work of art in the world. To this day, The Mona Lisa holds the Guinness World Record for the highest known insurance valuation in history... $650,000,000.

THE BIRTH OF VENUS - 1486
SANDRO BOTTICELLI

Painted during the Renaissance Florence period, hanging in Florence's Uffizi Gallery is the first work ever done on canvas. It is the 6 feet by 9 feet interpretation of The Birth of Venus by Sandro Botticelli.

His career as an artist was often overshadowed by the other artists of the High Renaissance. But 400 years after The Birth of Venus completion, Botticelli finally won esteem in the 19th century.

THE CREATION OF ADAM - 1548
MICHELANGELO BUONARROTI

The Creation of Adam is from Genesis, "God created man in His own image..." Michelangelo Buonarroti (1475—1564) had a vision of design that was rooted in the understanding of the human body. In 1990, a neurologist, Frank Meshberger, noted in the Journal of the American Medical Association that "the background figures and shapes portrayed behind the figure of God in The Creation of Adam appeared to be an anatomically accurate picture of the human brain. If you look closely at the painting, the borders correlate with the inner and outer surface of the brain, the brain stem, the frontal lobe, and the pituitary gland." Michelangelo, a supreme master of human anatomy, placed a graying bearded man portraying God inside the human brain secretly showing to the world that it is not "God created man in his own image" but Man creating God in his own image.

SISYPHUS - 1549
TITIAN

In 1548, Mary of Hungary, Charles V's sister, commissioned Titian to paint four large canvases of 'The Damned' depicting Tityus, Sisyphus, Tantalus, and Ixion all condemned to perpetual torture for incurring the displeasure of the gods. On 22 August 1549, to demonstrate the destiny of those who rise up against their legitimate rulers, Mary hung the large paintings in the Great Room in the Palace of Binche. She clothed her message in a mythological guise, comparing a challenge to the Gods with that of the German Princes to the Emperor.

JUDITH BEHEADING HOLOFERENES - 1607
MICHELANGELO MERSI DA CARAVAGGIO

Michelangelo Merisi da Caravaggio is generally credited with the invention of the tenebrism style which is violent contrasts of light and dark and where darkness becomes a dominating feature of the image. The technique was developed to add drama to an image through a spotlight effect and was popular in Baroque painting. Caravaggio's life was much like his paintings, violent contrasts of light and dark. In 1606 he brawled and killed a pimp over a woman which led to his death sentence for murder and he fled to Naples. In 1610, hoping for a papal pardon for his crime, he traveled to Rome by ship with several of his paintings. When the ship arrived, Caravaggio was arrested and was led away to the magistrate. As he watched the ship leave for Porto Ercole with his paintings, Caravaggio determined to get his paintings back, paid the large bond to get out of jail. However, in Porto Ercole on July 18, 1610, he became ill and died. The paintings were never recovered. However, in 2014, Caravaggio's Judith Beheading Holofernes was found in an attic in Toulouse, France.

SUSANNA AND THE ELDERS - 1610
ARTEMISIA GENTILESCHI

An oil painting by Italian female painter Artemisia Gentileschi, based on the Biblical story in the Book of Daniel, Susanna and the Elders is a painting showing the influence of Caravaggio and was completed when Artemisia was just 17 years old. The biblical story is about the time when Susanna had gone out to the garden one day for a bath and during that time Susanna's housekeeper let the two elders in and they found Susanna. The elders then demanded sexual favors from her. Susanna denied them but they threatened to ruin her reputation if she did not change her mind. The two elders kept their word and tried to ruin Susanna's reputation until a young man named Daniel intervened. He noticed that some of the details in the two elders' stories did not match up.

When they were questioned separately, their stories did not coincide and so Susanna's name was cleared. When Artemisia painted Susanna, she made Susanna awkward and uncomfortable. She also decided against the typical body type that is normally shown in many other versions of Susanna and the Elders paintings and went with a more classical style. By choosing a more classical style for Susanna's body, she created a heroic feeling. Since Artemisia painted this vertically, the elders are allowed to be spread out at the top, which turns them into a dark element hovering over the scene and creating a feeling of pressure on Susanna. However, it is also true that no other artist had ever before explored the psychological dimension of this Biblical story.

SAMSON AND DELILAH - 1610
SIR PETER PAUL RUBENS

"After intensive research I discovered what Delilah knew about her boyfriend Samson's hair. His prodigious strength and power came not from his never barbered hair but from the massive muscles in his arms and back."

- Carl Reiner

DANIEL IN THE LION'S DEN - 1616
SIR PETER PAUL RUBENS

One of the greatest masters of the 17th century masterfully combined realism and theatricality in order to draw a strong emotional reaction. Several lions, for instance, stare at us directly, suggesting that we share their space, and like Daniel, experience the same menace by portraying them close to life-size with convincing realism. The lions' lifelike movement and their superbly rendered fur resulted from Rubens's direct observation and sketches he made at the royal menagerie in Brussels. The dramatic lighting and the exaggerated emotionalism of Daniel's prayerful pose add to the veracity. This grand, powerful, and vivid image is unquestionably one of the artist's most memorable achievement.

THE LAUGHING CAVALIER - 1624
FRANS HALS

The Laughing Cavalier is a portrait by the Dutch Golden Age painter Frans Hals in the Wallace Collection in London, which has been described as "one of the most brilliant of all Baroque portraits". The title is an invention of the public and press dating from its 1872 exhibition at the Bethnal Green Museum in England, after which it was regularly produced as print. It became one of the best known old master paintings. The unknown subject is in fact not laughing, but can be said to have an enigmatic smile, much amplified by his upturned moustache.

THE NIGHT WATCH - 1642
REMBRANDT HARMENSZOON VAN RIJN

One of the greatest portrait paintings of the 17th century Dutch Baroque era is The Night Watch. A painting of colossal size (12 ft × 15 ft), it was executed by Rembrandt at the height of his career. Originally called The Company of Frans Banning Cocq and Willem van Ruytenburch, it is a group portrait of a militia company, commissioned and paid for by the members concerned, and was intended for the Great Room of the Kloveniersdoelen (the Musketeers Assembly Hall). Based on the 18th-century's false assumption that it depicted a nocturnal scene, The Night Watch was given its popular but misleading title. In fact, its subdued lighting was caused by the premature darkening of its multi-layered varnish. The picture was a huge success at the time, not least because it turns a fairly humdrum subject into a dynamic work of art. Unlike other Baroque portraits of militia companies, which traditionally portrayed members lined up in neat rows or sitting at a banquet, Rembrandt's painting shows the company fully equipped, ready for action, and about to march.

GIRL WITH A PEARL EARRING - 1665
JOHANNES VERMEER

Although now a highly regarded artist, Vermeer, during his lifetime, was not well known outside of his native city of Delft. Girl with a Pearl Earring became one of Vermeer's more famous pieces, and then around the turn of the 21st century, with the 1995 blockbuster exhibition at the National Gallery of Art, and the publication of Tracy Chevalier's best-selling novel, "Girl with a Pearl Earring." The author fashioned the painting's subject into a house-maid named Griet who worked in Vermeer's home and became his paint mixer. In 2003, the book was adapted into an Oscar-nominated film starring Scarlett Johansson as the fictional Griet and Colin Firth as Vermeer. As the Mauritshuis building, where the painting was on display, underwent renovation in 2012, Girl with a Pearl Earring traveled to Japan, Italy, and the United States. It drew crowds in each location, attesting to its now firm place in audience regard. In 2014 when 'Girl' returned to the Netherlands, the Mauritshuis stated it would no longer lend out the painting, assuring visitors it will always be on view in its home.

PORTRAIT OF PAUL REVERE - 1768
JOHN SINGLETON COPLEY

At age 41, Revere was a prosperous, established and prominent Boston silversmith. He had helped organize an intelligence and alarm system to keep watch on the British military. He is best known for his midnight ride to alert the colonial militia in April 1775 to the approach of British forces before the battles of Lexington and Concord, as dramatized in Henry Wadsworth Longfellow's poem, "Paul Revere's Ride". Revere's daughter Harriet so disliked the Copley portrait because of its informality she relegated it to the attic. However, in 1861, Longfellow published his poem "Paul Revere's Ride," creating an interest in the portrait. The Revere family had the painting restored but not publicly displayed until 1928, when it was loaned to the Museum of Fine Arts in Boston. In 1930, his great-grandsons donated the painting to the Museum.

THE BLUE BOY - 1770
THOMAS GAINSBOROUGH

In 1770 Thomas Gainsborough had high hopes for the piece's reception when it debuted at the Royal Academy, a prestigious venue for any artist. The incredible play of colour and brush strokes of The Blue Boy made it an instantly adored hit.

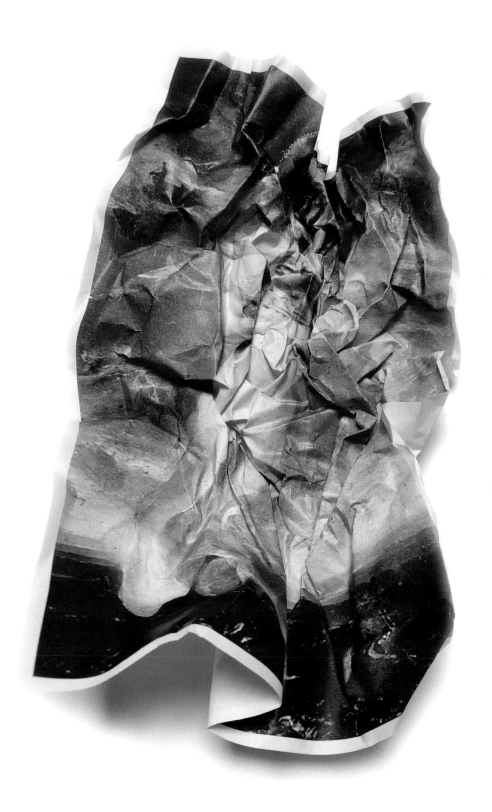

Pinkie (Sarah Barrett Moulton) - 1795
Thomas Lawrence

Pinkie hangs opposite The Blue Boy in the permanent collection of the Huntington Library at San Marino, California. The title "Pinkie" came from Sarah's grandmother asking her niece, the famous poet Elizabeth Barrett Browning to commission a portrait, 'I must beg a favor, I miss my dear little Pinkey so much since she is attending Ms. Fenwick's school in Greenwich. Can you please have a portrait done at full length by one of the best masters, please tell them to capture Sarah's easy, carefree attitude.'

Ms. Browning appointed Thomas Lawrence who was the portrait artist in residence for George III. The depiction of the eleven year old Sarah Barrett Moulton with a playful direct gaze and the energetic brushwork of Lawrence captured the essence of the young girl. The painting was finished in April 1795, but Sarah never got to see the final work because she became very ill with a severe flu. Ms. Browning delivered the painting to Sarah's grandmother on the day Sarah died.

THE DEATH OF MARAT - 1795
JACQUES - LOUIS DAVID

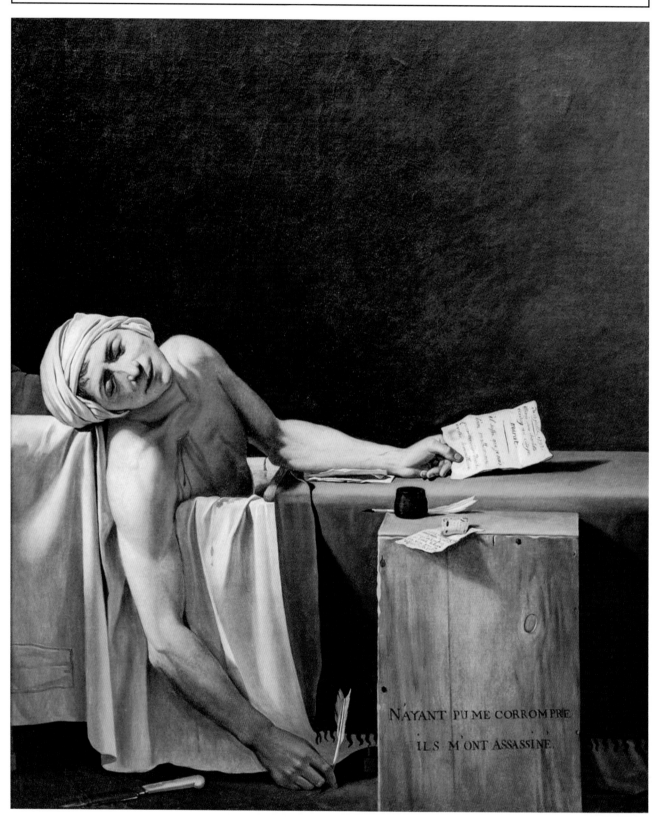

NAYANT PU ME CORROMPRE

ILS M'ONT ASSASSINE.

The Death of Marat (French: La Mort de Marat or Marat Assassiné) is a painting of the murdered French revolutionary leader Jean-Paul Marat. It is one of the most famous images of the French Revolution.

David was a leading French painter, as well as a member of the Revolutionary Committee. The painting shows the radical journalist lying dead in his bath on July 13, 1793, after being murdered by Charlotte Corday.

FISHERMEN AT SEA - 1796
JOSEPH MALLORD WILLIAM TURNER

In 1796, Turner just turned 21 when he completed Fishermen at Sea, which was acclaimed by the Royal Academy of Art as the work "of an original mind". Turner was accepted into the Academy, where he lectured until 1828. The potency of the moonlight contrasts with the delicate vulnerability of the flickering lantern. It emphasized nature's power over mankind and the fishermen's fate. The jagged silhouettes on the left are the treacherous rocks called 'the Needles' off the Isle of Wight. Many consider Turner to be the father of impressionism.

Napoleon Crossing the Alps - 1805
Jacques - Louis David

The portrait was commissioned by Charles IV of Spain. It is housed in Madrid's Royal Palace with paintings of other great military leaders. The composition shows a strongly idealized view of Napoleon and his army crossing the Alps. In May 1800, Napolean led his troops across the Great St. Bernard Pass in a military campaign against the Austrians which ended in the Austrians' defeat in June at the Battle of Marengo. However...

BONAPARTE CROSSING THE ALPS
PAUL DELAROCHE

Jacques-Louis David's version of the scene differs a great deal from Paul Delaroche's idea of Napoleon's crossing of the Alps. Arthur George, Third Earl of Onslow, visited the Louvre in Paris where he saw David's version of the famous event. George, who owned a sizable collection of Napoleonic paraphernalia, felt that the painting was unrealistic and commissioned Delaroche to create a more realistic depiction of the true story. Napolean chose to ride across the alps on a mule rather than a steed, the typical gentleman's mount, because the mule was more sure-footed on the Alps' slippery slopes and narrow passes. Both George and Delaroche agreed to depict Napoleon as a credible man, who suffered and underwent human hardship too, and felt that making him appear as he really would have been in the situation would by no means debase or diminish Napoleon iconic status, but rather a more admirable person.

WANDERER ABOVE THE SEA OF FOG - 1818
CASPAR DAVID FRIEDRICH

Some believe Wanderer Above the Sea of Fog to be a self portrait of Friedrich. The young figure standing in contemplation has the same fiery red hair as the artist. Friedrich famously once said, "The artist should not only paint what he sees before him, but also what he sees within him." In his eyes, contemplation of and emotional response to nature was of primary interest. After wedding Caroline Bommer in 1818, with whom he had three children, Friedrich's paintings saw use of a brighter and less austere palette and conveyed a sense of levity. However, in 1835, he suffered a stroke and his paralysis limited his abilities, making him more melancholic. Toward the end of his life, Friedrich was living as a recluse. His friends called him "the most solitary of the solitary". He died in relative poverty.

LIBERTY LEADING THE PEOPLE - 1830
EUGENE DELACROIX

Liberty Leading the People by Eugène Delacroix commemorates the July Revolution of 1830, which toppled King Charles X of France. Marianne, a woman personifying the goddess of Liberty, viewed as a symbol of France, leads the people forward holding the flag of the French Revolution stepping over the dedicated fallen— the tricolour flag, which remains France's flag in one hand and brandishing a bayonetted musket with the other.

THE GREAT WAVE - 1833
KATSUSHIKA HOKUSAI

The Great Wave is Hokusai's most famous paining and one of the most recognizable works of Japanese art in the world. The image depicts an enormous wave threatening three boats off the coast of the town of Kanagawa (the present-day city of Yokohama, Kanagawa Prefecture) while Mount Fuji rises in the center.

The wave is assumed to be a tsunami, however it is more likely to be a large rogue wave. Like many of the prints in the series, it depicts the area around Mount Fuji under particular conditions, and the mountain itself appears in the background. Throughout the series are dramatic uses of Berlin blue pigment.

WASHINGTON CROSSING THE DELAWARE - 1851
EMANUEL GOTTLIEB LEUTZE

Washington Crossing the Delaware is an 1851 oil-on-canvas painting by the German American artist Emanuel Gottlieb Leutze. It commemorates General George Washington's crossing of the Delaware River on the night of December 25–26, 1776, during the American Revolutionary War. That action was the first move in a surprise attack against the Hessian forces at Trenton, New Jersey. In WWII the original was part of the collection at the Kunsthalle in Bremen, Germany and was destroyed in a British air raid. Leutze painted two more versions, one of which is now in the Metropolitan Museum of Art in New York City.

OPHELIA - 1852
SIR JOHN EVERETT MILLAIS

The scene depicted is from Shakespeare's Hamlet, Act IV, Scene vii, in which Ophelia, driven out of her mind when her father is murdered by her lover Hamlet, falls into a stream and drowns:

There is a willow grows aslant a brook,
That shows his hoar leaves in the glassy stream;
There with fantastic garlands did she come
Of crow-flowers, nettles, daisies, and long purples
That liberal shepherds give a grosser name,
But our cold maids do dead men's fingers call them:
There, on the pendent boughs her coronet weeds
Clambering to hang, an envious sliver broke;
When down her weedy trophies and herself
Fell in the weeping brook. Her clothes spread wide;
And, mermaid-like, awhile they bore her up:
Which time she chanted snatches of old tunes;
As one incapable of her own distress,
Or like a creature native and indued
Unto that element: but long it could not be
Till that her garments, heavy with their drink,
Pull'd the poor wretch from her melodious lay
To muddy death.

ARRANGEMENT IN GREY AND BLACK, No. 1 - 1871
JAMES MCNEILL WHISTLER

Arrangement in Grey and Black, No. 1. is the painting's real title but became known as "Whistler's Mother". Anna Matilda McNeill Whistler, who lived with him in London from 1864 to 1875. Anna sits in profile with an air of infinite patience. It became the first American art work ever bought by the French state, and it remains the most important American work residing outside the United States. Along with The Mona Lisa and Girl With a Pearl Earring, "Whistler's Mother" became an instant pin-up of popular art. It was sheer happenstance that Anna Matilda became famous because she had agreed to sit for it when the young model he had hired failed to show up.

BAL DU MOULIN DE LA GALETTE - 1871
PIERRE -AUGUSTE RENOIR

Bal du Moulin de la Galette, the Paris café and dancehall, was painted in 1871 by the pioneer Impressionist Pierre-Auguste Renoir who attended Sunday afternoon dances and where he enjoyed watching the happy couples. This celebrated masterpiece is the fifth most expensive painting ever sold and now resides in its present home at Le Musee d'Orsay.

THE DANCE CLASS - 1874
EDGAR DEGAS

In The Dance Class, Edgar Degas depicts a candid scene of ballerinas, and he does not focus on the great whirl of movement and colour created by the dancers. Rather, Degas chose to explore the form of the ballerina in her brief moments of respite, capturing the ungraceful realism of human gesture.

BOATING - 1874
EDOUARD MANET

In 1874, Manet summered at Gennevilliers, often spending time with Monet and Renoir across the Seine at Argenteuil, where Boating was painted. By not adopting the lighter touch of his younger ambitious Impressionist colleagues, Manet exploited a different use of colour and used similar strong diagonals of Japanese prints to give inimitable form to this scene of outdoor leisure. Rodolphe Leenhoff, the artist's brother-in-law, is thought to have posed for the sailor but the identity of the woman is uncertain.

IMPRESSION, SUNRISE - 1874
CLAUDE MONET

Claude Monet depicts the harbour at Le Havre as the sun rises over the cranes, derricks and masts of the anchored ships. Standing at a window overlooking the harbour the artist captured the early morning mist, and industrial smoke.

The only evidence of life is the oarsman, the most defined part of the painting. The composition, though simple, like most Impressionist paintings, is balanced by the reflection of the sun in the water.

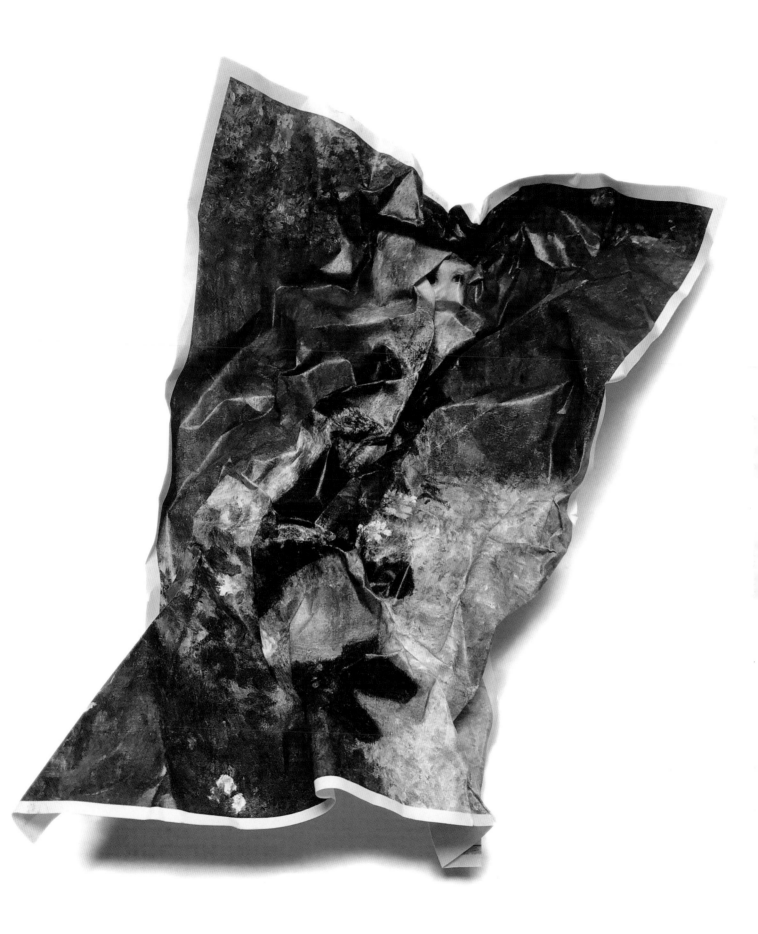

THE GIRL WITH A WATERING CAN - 1876
PIERRE-AUGUSTE RENOIR

The girl in this painting is a girl that lived near Renoir, named Mademoiselle Leclere. He picked her because of her doll-like features and especially her distinctive eyes. This painting is a classical Impressionist painting, as it focuses on the different colours and how they can be used to represent the effects of sunlight. Like many other Impressionist paintings, this work was painted while Renoir was outside (something that was uncommon in the period before Impressionism). However, at the same time, the simplicity of this painting is a first step in the direction of Post-Impressionism.

BREEZING UP - 1876
WINSLOW HOMER

Breezing Up was originally the title of a watercolour sketch Winslow Homer had done while visiting in Gloucester, Massachusetts. Choosing, from a number of sketches, he re-painted the sketch in oil, changing the composition somewhat. Keeping the same title, it is considered his finest iconic American painting, and is currently housed at the National Gallery of Art in Washington D.C.

Paris Street; Rainy Day - 1877
Gustave Caillebotte

The painting was first shown at the Impressionist Exhibition of 1877. It is currently owned by the Art Institute of Chicago. AIC curator Gloria Groom described the work as "the great picture of urban life in the late 19th century". Although Caillebotte was a friend and patron of the Impressionists, and this work is part of that school, it differs in its realism and reliance on line rather than broad brush strokes. Caillebotte's interest in photography is evident. The figures in the foreground appear "out of focus," those in the mid-distance (the carriage and the pedestrians) have sharp edges, while the features in the background become progressively indistinct. The severe cropping of some figures – particularly the man to the far right – further suggests the influence of photography.

Renoir portrayed the two daughters of Louise Cahen d'Anvers... the blonde, Elisabeth, born in December 1874, and the younger, Alice, in February 1876. The artist produced many portraits for the Parisian Jewish community at the time.

64

A Bar at the Folies-Bergère - 1882
Edouard Manet

A Bar at the Folies-Bergère, painted and exhibited at the Paris Salon in 1882, is considered the last major work of French painter Édouard Manet. The painting originally belonged to the composer Emmanuel Chabrier, who hung it over his piano. Chabrier was a close friend of Manet and the painting is currently in The Courtauld Institute of Art in London.

A SUNDAY AFTERNOON ON THE ISLAND
OF LA GRANDE JATTE - 1884
GEORGES SEURAT

In 1881, Seurat opened a small studio in Paris. While continuing his studies on the tonal effects of colour, with a series of conte crayon drawings, he developed an intellectual style of painting that would open up new possibilities for art. The technique he settled on, nicknamed 'Pointillism,' involved the use of small touches of pure colour, which are not mixed but placed side by side on the canvas. When viewed from a certain distance, these touches of colour blend together.

ROBERT LOUIS STEVENSON - 1887
JOHN SINGER SARGENT

Stevenson, in frail health at the time, was anchored in the stable wicker chair. His lankiness remains evident in his long, crossed legs, which extend to the edge of the frame. Amid this stillness, Sargent, painted a lush carpet with energetic dabs, painted a lush carpet. Boston banker Charles Fairchild commissioned the work as a gift for his wife, who was an ardent fan of the author.

THE LADY OF SHALOTT-1888
JOHN WILLIAM WATERHOUSE

The Lady of Shalott based on the figure of Lady Elaine of Astolat from medieval Arthurian legend is an oil painting of a scene from Tennyson's poem in which he depicted the plight of a young woman who yearned with an unrequited love for Knight Sir Lancelot. It is one of John William Waterhouse's most famous works.

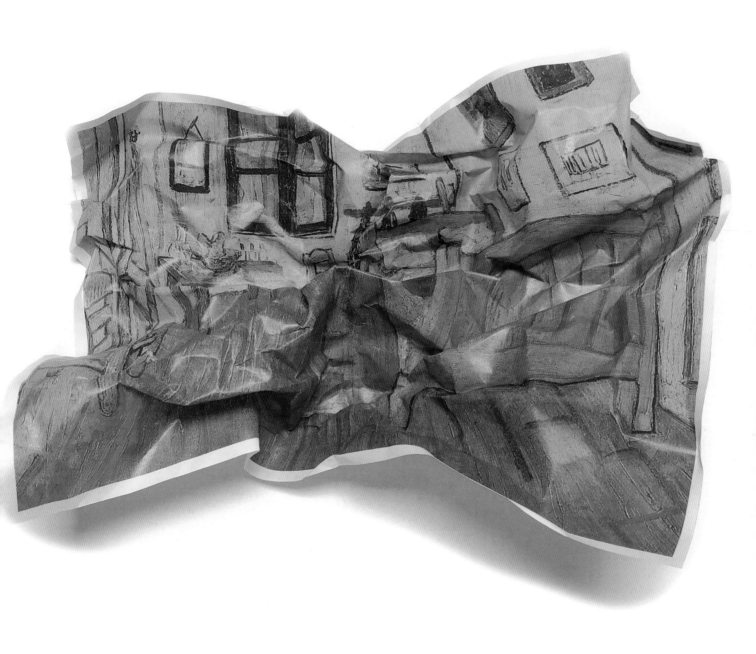

THE BEDROOM - 1888

VINCENT VAN GOGH

From an October 16, 1888 letter from Vincent to his brother Theo:

My dear Theo,

At last I'm sending you a little croquis to give you at least an idea of the direction the work is taking... This time it's simply my bedroom, but the colour has to do the job here... The walls are of a pale violet. The floor is of red tiles. the bedstead and the chairs are fresh butter yellow. The sheet and the pillows very bright lemon green. The blanket scarlet red. The window green. The dressing table orange, the basin blue. The doors lilac. And that's all... The solidity of the furniture should also now express unshakable repose... The frame... will be white. This to take my revenge for the enforced rest that I was obliged to take... How are your pains? Don't forget to give me news about them... I shake your hand firmly.

Ever yours,

Vincent

THE STARRY NIGHT - 1889
VINCENT VAN GOGH

In June 1889 Van Gogh painted The Starry Night, one of 21 versions that depicts the view from the east-facing window of his asylum room at Saint-Rémy-de-Provence. He wrote to his brother, Theo, and offered him a rare nighttime glimpse into what he saw in isolation. "Through the iron-barred window I can make out a square of wheat in an enclosure, above which in the morning I see the sun rise in its glory," Van Gogh wrote. "I have done another landscape with olive trees, and a new study of the 'starry sky.'"

SELF PORTRAIT-1889
VINCENT VAN GOGH

This is one of many self-portraits. He used oil on canvas to paint this particular piece. Vincent Van Gogh painted it in September 1889, shortly before he left the asylum at Saint-Rémy-de-Provence in southern France.

AT THE MOULIN ROUGE: THE DANCE - 1890
HENRI DE TOULOUSE - LAUTREC

Here, Toulouse-Lautrec captures the energy and seedy underbelly of Paris night life. Through an opening in the crowd, we glimpse the center of the Moulin-Rouge. A dancer in mid-kick lifts her skirt above her knees (revealing much more leg than was considered ladylike), while a more modestly dressed, well-heeled woman with an upturned nose looks on, disapprovingly. Yet why is she in this space? What is she looking for? Toulouse-Lautrec was a great observer of night life, with its cast of characters: entertainers, dandies, and ladies of the night. The composition is like a spinning top with the female dancer at its center. Toulouse-Lautrec uses colour to move the eye outward across the painting, from the pink dress to the red stockings, and over to a red blazer in the background, drawing us right into the action.

PORTRAIT OF DR. GACHET-1893
VINCENT VAN GOGH

Portrait of Dr. Gachet depicts a very relaxed Dr. Paul Gachet, Vincent's true friend who took care of him during the final months of his life. In 1890, Van Gogh's brother Theo was searching for a home for the artist upon his release from an asylum at Saint-Rémy. Upon the recommendation of Camille Pissarro, a former patient of the doctor who told Theo of Gachet's interests in working with artists, Theo sent Vincent to Gachet's second home in Auvers. In 1990, this painting fetched a record price of $82.5 million when auctioned at Christie's New York. Bidding began at $20 million and quickly jumped skyward in million-dollar increments. The numbers kept escalating as new bidders entered the competition, including Hideto Kobayashi, head of the Kobayashi Gallery of Tokyo, who ultimately raised his hand for the winning bid.

MADAME X - 1893
JOHN SINGER SARGENT

John Singer Sargent enjoyed international acclaim as a portrait painter. In the beginning, his work is characterized by remarkable technical facility, particularly in his ability to draw with a brush, which in later years inspired admiration as well as criticism for a supposed superficiality. His commissioned works were consistent with the grand manner of portraiture, while his informal studies and landscape paintings displayed a familiarity with Impressionism. In later life Sargent expressed ambivalence about the restrictions of formal portrait work, and devoted much of his energy to mural painting and working "in plain air". Until the late 20th century, historians generally ignored "society" artists such as Sargent.

THE CHILD'S BATH - 1893
MARY CASSATT

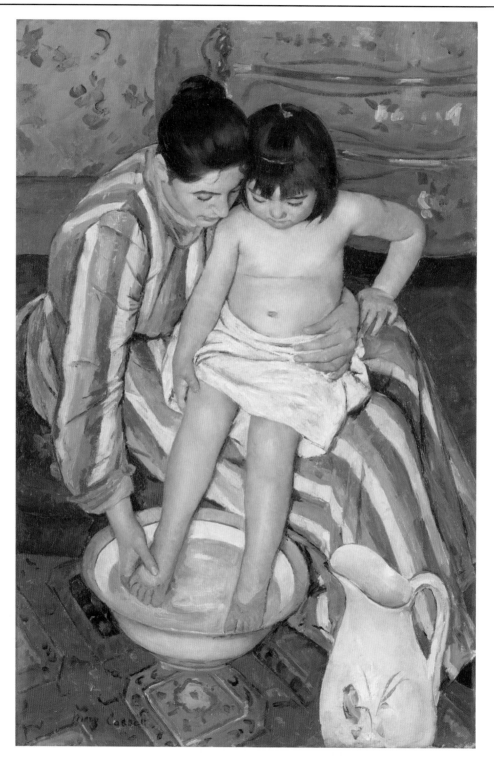

Mary Cassatt was the only American to exhibit with the Impressionist group. Like her friend Degas, she was a highly skilled draftsman who preferred unposed, asymmetrical compositions. During and after the 1880s, the theme of women caring for children appeared frequently in Cassatt's art. She depicted children being bathed, dressed, read to, held, or nursed, reflecting the most advanced 19th-century idea about raising children. After 1870, French scientists and physicians encouraged mothers (instead of wet-nurses and nannies) to care for their children and suggested modern approaches to health and personal hygiene, including regular bathing. In the mid-1880s, in the face of several cholera epidemics, bathing was encouraged, not only as a remedy for body odors, but also as a preventative measure against disease.

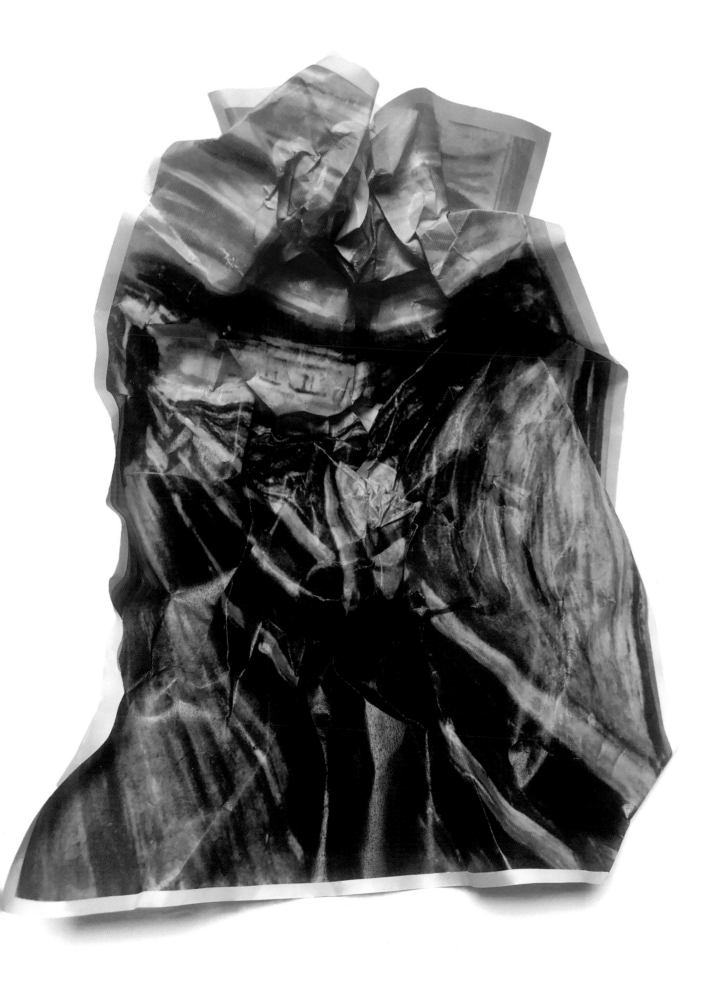

THE SCREAM - 1893
EDVARD MUNCH

"I was walking down the road with two friends when the sun set; suddenly, the sky turned as red as blood. I stopped and leaned against the fence, feeling unspeakably tired. Tongues of fire and blood stretched over the bluish black fjord. My friends went on walking, while I lagged behind, shivering with fear. Then I heard the enormous infinite scream of nature."

- Edvard Munch

The Scream, painted during a unique transitional period in art history, "Fin de Siecle". Artists were interested in painting their subjects objectively, since their success was often measured by their technical skill.

By the end of the nineteenth century, brave artists like Edvard Munch were starting to use art by painting with bright, exaggerated colours and simple shapes to express their inner thoughts, feelings, and emotions.

THE CARD PLAYERS - 1895
PAUL CEZANNE

The Card Players is a series of five oil paintings. Paul Cézanne is said to have formed the bridge between late 19th-century Impressionism and the early 20th century's new line of artistic enquiry, Cubism. The paintings convey Cézanne's intense study of his subjects. Manet, Matisse, and Picasso are said to have remarked that Cézanne "is the father of all of us".

The scene has been described as balanced but asymmetrical, as well as naturally symmetrical with the two players being each other's "partner in an agreed opposition". In each of the two-player paintings, a sole wine bottle rests in the mid-part of the table, said to represent a dividing line between the two participants as well as the center of the painting's "symmetrical balance".

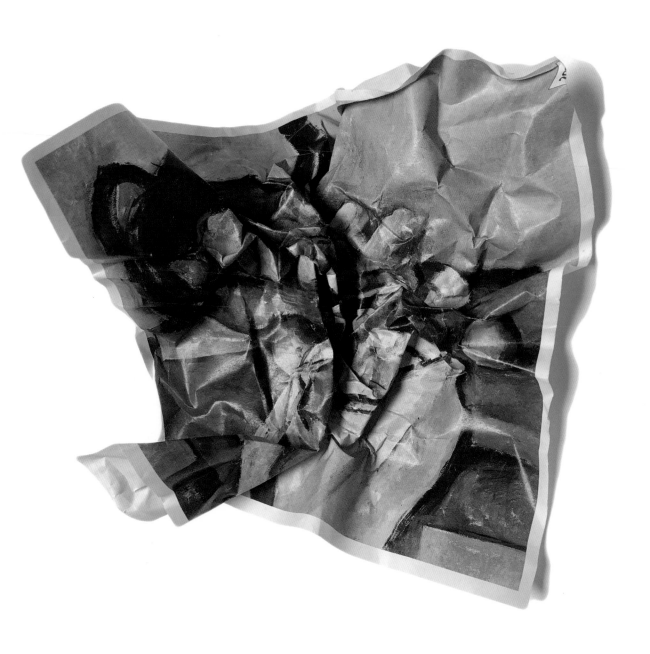

THE BASKET OF APPLES - 1895
PAUL CĒZANNE

The Basket of Apples is a still life oil painting by French artist Paul Cézanne. The piece is often noted for its disjointed perspective. It has been described as a balanced composition due to its unbalanced parts; the tilted bottle, the incline of the basket, and the foreshortened lines of the cookies mesh with the lines of the tablecloth. Additionally, the right side of the tabletop is not in the same plane as the left side, as if the image simultaneously reflects two viewpoints. Paintings such as this helped form a bridge between Impressionism and Cubism.

FLAMING JUNE - 1895
FREDERIC LEIGHTON

Flaming June has become Leighton's most recognizable picture. Samuel Courtauld, founder of the Courtauld Institute, called it "the most wonderful painting in existence". The realism of the transparent material worn by the sleeping woman, the stunningly rich colours and the perfectly recreated marble, and his use of natural light are characteristic of Leighton's work. He allows the sunset in the background to appear as molten gold.

THE SLEEPING GYPSY - 1897
HENRI ROUSSEAU

The Sleeping Gypsy is an 1897 oil painting by French Naïve artist Henri Rousseau. It is a fantastical depiction of a moonlit night with a lion musing over a sleeping woman. Rousseau first exhibited the painting at the 13th Salon des Indépendants, and tried unsuccessfully to sell it to the mayor of his hometown, Laval. Instead, the painting entered the private collection of a Parisian charcoal merchant, where it remained until 1924 when it was discovered by the art critic Louis Vauxcelles.

LE BOULEVARD DE MONTMARTRE
MATINEE DE PRINTEMPS - 1897
CAMILLE PISSARRO

Jacob Abraham Camille Pissarro was born on 10 July 1830 on the island of St. Thomas to Frederick and Rachel Manzano de Pissarro. His father was of Portuguese Jewish descent and held French nationality. His mother was from a French-Jewish family from the island of St. Thomas. After spending six years in a small village in Northern France, Pissarro returned to Paris, where he painted several series of the grand boulevard that he surveyed from his lodgings at the Grand Hotel de Russie. Pissarro marveled that he could see down the whole length of the boulevard with the spectacle of urban life as it unfolded below his window.

THE WATER-LILY POND - 1899
CLAUDE MONET

This reflective painting of the lily pond with its dappled sunlight and its orchestration of colour, tone and texture was one out of a series of twelve. With the invention of the flat, square, ferrule paintbrush, as opposed to the round brush, Monet was able to use short rapid brushstrokes to create the water's flower-laden surface. With his palette knife, he applied layers of paint until a thick crust was formed, capturing the textures and shapes of the foliage.

TWO TAHITIAN WOMEN – 1899
PAUL GAUGIN

Gauguin's work in Tahiti focused on the beauty and serene virtues of the native women. He depended on sculpturally modeled forms, gesture, and facial expression to vivify the sentiments. He described the "Tahitian Eve" as being very knowing of her naïveté but still capable of walking around naked, seemingly without shame.

L' ENFANT AU PIGEON - 1901
PABLO PICASSO

Pablo Picasso was a Spanish expatriate painter, sculptor, printmaker, ceramicist, and stage designer, one of the greatest and most-influential artists of the 20th century, and the creator (with Georges Braque) of Cubism.

Child with a Dove is one of Picasso's earliest works: he was twenty-one when he broke out with a new thoughtfulness, a poetic sympathy with the subject, qualities that were to dominate his work in the years that followed.

LA VIE - 1903
PABLO PICASSO

In 1901, Picasso launched into the melancholic paintings that formed his Blue Period during the years between 1901 to 1904. What triggered this period is when Pablo and his close friend, Carlos Casegamas, left the "conservative" art school in Spain for the city of lights, (Paris, France) to pursue their dreams as unfettered artists. However, tragedy struck when Casegemas had fallen in love with the beautiful Germaine Pichot, an artist's model, but his love was unrequited, due to his impotence. Germaine had rejected Casegamas. On February 17th, 1901, Casagemas was dining with Germaine and friends in L'Hippodrome Café when he attempted to shoot Germaine but failed. He then turned the revolver and shot himself in the right temple. The painting of La Vie took till 1903 for Picasso to fully comprehend what had happened to his best friend. Thus La Vie came into existence when Picasso recreated the moment when Germaine discovers Casegemas' impotence which is hinted by the placement of the loin cloth. The presence of the woman with a child has been said by Picasso to represent life and death... "The mother is always present in a person's life from birth to death." Picasso uses the mother figure again in "The Tragedy".

THE TRAGEDY - 1903
PABLO PICASSO

With The Tragedy his obsession with themes of human misery and social alienation reached its climax. Picasso often described his adventure with his best friend, Carlos Casegemas, as two youngmen setting sail into the unknown when they left art school for Paris... Anything could happen to them... Thus The Tragedy was created of a journey gone horribly wrong only to wash up on a strange shore without any help or hope for the future. The mother with child again appears in this painting as the harbinger of death. The castaways on this unknown shore became the metaphor that Picasso was searching for and with it the climax of Picasso's blue period.

THE OLD GUITARIST-1903
PABLO PICASSO

The Old Guitarist was painted in 1903, just after the suicide death of Picasso's close friend, Casagemas. During this time, the artist was sympathetic to the plight of the downtrodden and painted many canvases depicting the miseries of the poor, the ill, and those cast out of society. He also knew what it was like to be impoverished, having been nearly penniless during all of 1902. This work was created in Madrid, and the distorted style (note that the upper torso of the guitarist seems to be reclining, while the bottom half appears to be sitting cross-legged) is reminiscent of the works of El Greco.

THE SCOUT: FRIENDS OR FOES? - 1905
FREDERIC REMINGTON

Frederic Remington was an American artist who specialized in depictions of the American Old West, specifically concentrating on scenes from the last quarter of the 19th century in the Western United States. Remington featured and romanticized images from Western culture, sketching cowboys, American Indians, and the U.S. Cavalry in the field. Then he would return home to his studio in New Rochelle, NY, where he completed most of his great work.

LA FENETRE OUVERTE - 1905
HENRI MATISSE

The beauty of Open Window contains a dazzling variety of colour and brush strokes from long blended marks to short, staccato touches. Matisse represented each area of the image - the interior of the room, the window itself, the balcony, the harbor view - with a distinctly different handling of the brush.

AU LAPIN AGILE - 1905
PABLO PICASSO

In this celebrated work, now an icon of life in bohemian Paris at the turn of the last century, Picasso depicts himself dressed as a Harlequin accompanied by his recent lover, Germaine Pichot. Previously, she had been the fatal obsession of Picasso's great friend Carlos Casagemas, who, in 1901, committed suicide. The painting was commissioned by Frédé Gérard—seen playing guitar in the background. For his Montmartre cabaret, Picasso's "Le Lapin Agile" was, from 1905 until 1912, on permanent view in Paris, until it was sold to a German collector.

Note: In the 1970's my wife, Estelle, and I had the opportunity to enjoy a meal at one of the original tables at the famed "Au Lapin Agile."

LES DEMOISELLES D'AVIGNON - 1907
PABLO PICASSO

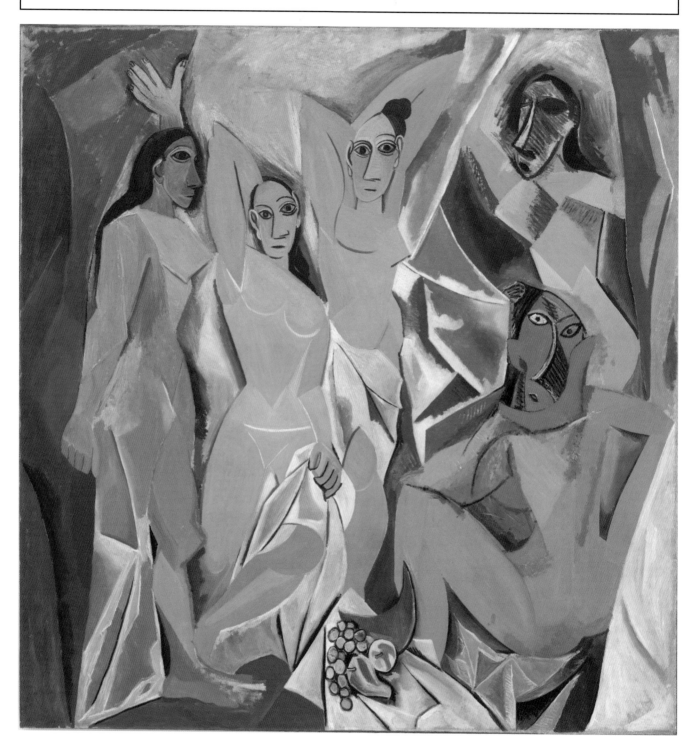

The form was revolutionary because it was not a naturalistic recreation of the way we see the world. It shows the distortion of the female body with the use of geometric shapes while questioning the expectations of idealized beauty of the past—further highlighted by the mask-like features of the two women on the farthest right.

Critics have hailed the painting as a watershed moment in art history, the first true work of both Cubism and of modern art. Picasso captured his vision on this canvas; and in 1907, he created the cultural break that divided the past and the future. Today the iconic work hangs in the Museum of Modern Art's permanent gallery.

THE KISS - 1907
GUSTAV KLIMT

The Kiss constitutes the height of Gustav Klimt's "Golden Phase," where his father's occupation as a goldsmith, ignited his taste for the element. Having familiarized himself with this trade, Klimt used a powdered gold coating, where he created a shimmering background acting as a golden cocoon for the lovers.

HANS TIETZE AND ERICA TIETZE-CONRAT-1909
OSKAR KOKOSCHKA

In 1909, the Viennese art historians Hans and Erica Tietze asked 23-year-old Oskar Kokoschka to paint a marriage portrait for their mantelpiece. The Tietzes were strong avid supporters of Viennese contemporary art and together helped organize the Vienna Society for the Advancement of Contemporary Art. Erica Tietze recalled that Kokoschka painted her and her husband separately, a fact suggested by the sense of separation between the couple and their strikingly distinct poses. Kokoschka used thin layers of colour to create the hazy surrounding atmosphere and added crackling energy to the composition by scratching into the paint with his fingernails.

THE GOLDFISH - 1912
HENRI MATISSE

In 1912, during his visit to Tangier, Morocco, Henri Matisse became fascinated with goldfish. He noted how the local population would daydream for hours, gazing into goldfish bowls.

NUDE DESCENDING A STAIRCASE - 1912
MARCEL DUCHAMP

In 1912, Duchamp's first work was created to provoke significant controversy in Nude Descending a Staircase, No. 2. The painting depicts the mechanistic motion of a nude, with superimposed facets, similar to motion pictures, showing elements of both the fragmentation and synthesis of the Cubists, and the dynamism of the Futurists.

THE BIRTHDAY - 1915
MARC CHAGALL

Marc Chagall called "love" the primary colour of his paintings. He met his wife, Bella, as a teenager in their home town of Vitebsk, Belarus. In 1915, despite the opposition of her parents, Chagall married Bella, who became the central source of love in his life. The Birthday was painted by Chagall just a few weeks before taking their vows.

The painting depicts the flowing and powerful love these two shared. Chagall is pictured flowing and dream-like, floating above Bella. As he twists around to kiss his future wife, he painted himself craning his head upside down and backward. Chagall's painting was wildly received because it broke away from the current traditions.

NUDE SITTING ON A DIVAN - 1917
AMEDEO MODIGLIANI

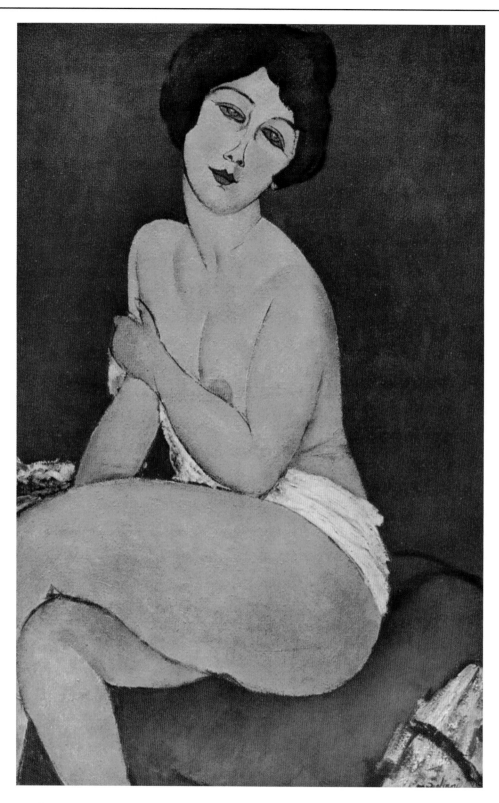

Nude Sitting on a Divan, an oil on canvas painting by Italian Jewish artist Amedeo Modigliani, was one of a series of nudes painted by Modigliani. In 1917, when exhibited in Paris, it created a sensation. During his short life, it was Modigliani's only solo exhibition and is "notorious" in modern art history for its sensational public reception and the attendant issues of obscenity. The show was closed by police on its opening day. Modigliani had little success while alive, and at the age of 35, two years after this opening, he died of tubercular meningitis. In 2010, this painting sold at a New York auction for the record price of a Modigliani at $68.9 million.

FAREWELL TO HAMBURG - 1921
OTTO DIX

In the summer of 1921, Otto Dix visited the port city of Hamburg on the North Sea. As he walked along the waterfront, he saw sailors on leave as they searched for pleasure on land. Along the red light district, Dix found brothels and prostitutes in abundance, a scene that may have helped reinforce earlier prejudices. During the war, Dix often held sailors in contempt.

The High Seas Fleet was in harbor for much of the conflict. From the artist's perspective, its sailors were chasing prostitutes and drinking gratuitous amounts of alcohol while the Wehrmacht bore the brunt of the war's burden. Dix's interpretation of a sailor's life as a string of exotic encounters has been described by Ashley Bassie in Expressionism as "intentionally kitch".

THREE MUSICIANS - 1921
PABLO PICASSO

Three Musicians is a perfect example of the Cubist style. In Cubism, the subject is transformed into a sequence of planes, lines, and arcs. It was described as an intellectual art form because the artist analyzes the shapes of their subjects and reinvents them on the canvas. Through this process, the viewer participates with Picasso in making sense of his artwork.

Le Petit Pâtissier - 1922
Chaim Soutine

In May 2013, Le Petit Pâtissier was sold for $18 million. It was a top lot and became the artist's most expensive painting. This work was the culminating image in a series of six different portraits of young pastry chefs in Paris.

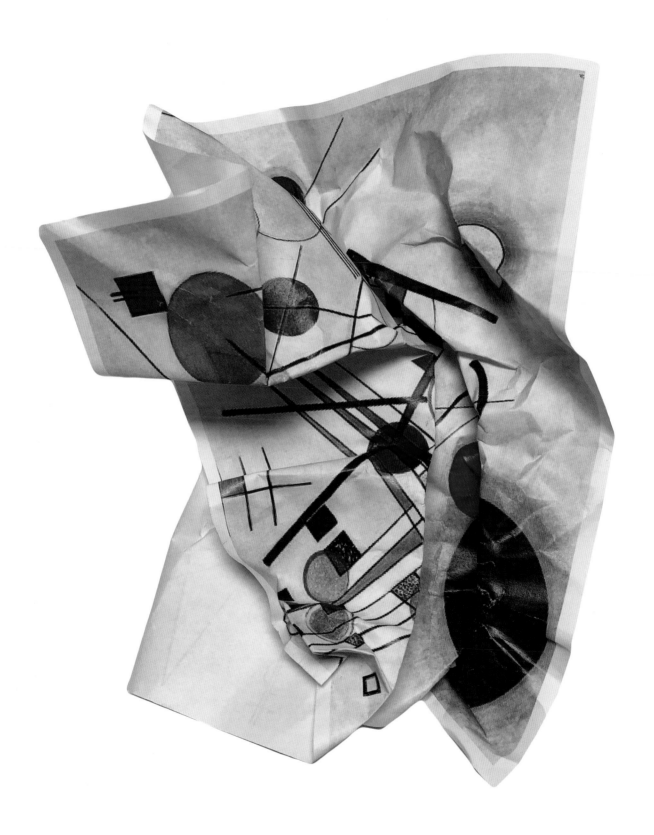

COMPOSITION VIII - 1923
VASSILY KANDINSKY

Kandinsky regarded Composition 8 as the high point of his post-World War I achievement. In this work, circles, triangles, and linear elements create a surface of interacting geometric forms creating dynamic compositional elements resembling mountains, sun, and atmosphere. In 1922,

Kandinsky was invited to become a faculty member at Bauhaus, where he discovered an environment that embraced his sensibilty. He taught there until 1933, when the Nazi government closed the Bauhaus and confiscated 57 of Kandinsky's works in its purge of "degenerate art".

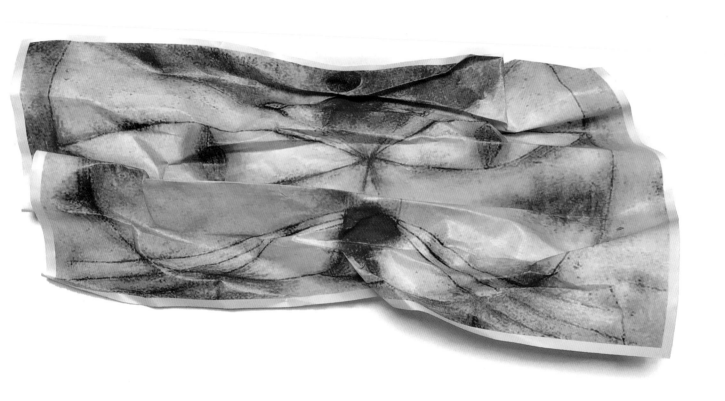

CAT AND BIRD - 1928
PAUL KLEE

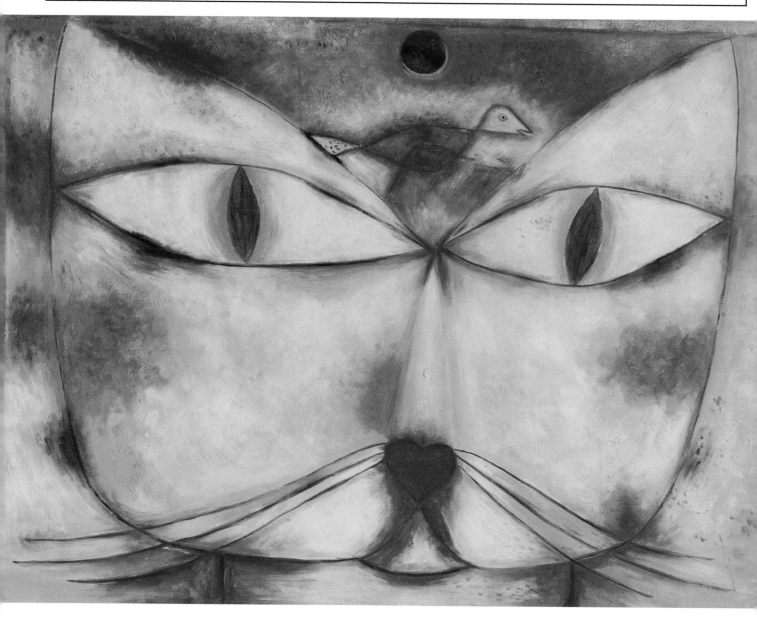

Klee, using line, shape, and colour for their own sake rather than to describe something visible, was one of the many modernist artists who wanted to practice what he called "the pure cultivation of the means" of painting. This freed him to create images dealing more with thought than with perception.

The bird in this picture seems to fly not in front of the cat's forehead but inside it—the bird is literally on the cat's mind. Stressing this point by making the cat all head, Klee concentrates on thought, fantasy, appetite, and the hungers of the brain. As an artist, one of Klee's aims was to "make secret visions visible".

THE LOVERS II - 1928
RENĒ MAGRITTE

The most significant aspect of The Lovers II is the veils. It is actually a rather bland painting, however, by simply covering the faces with veils it becomes far more interesting. Magritte called this painting the kiss of denied love. Their faces covered by a white cloth, they are locked in an ambiguous setting, and unable to truly communicate or touch. The cloth keeps the two figures forever apart, creating an atmosphere of mystery which celebrated this image. The way the room is painted makes it seem almost insignificant, no windows to give perspective of time.

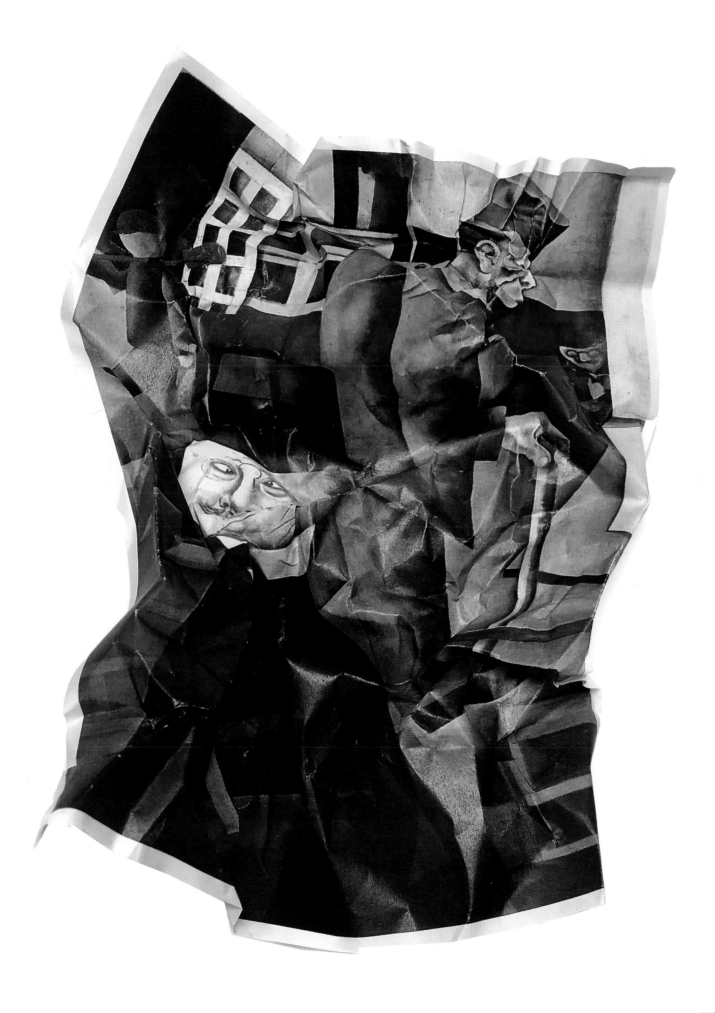

A GREY DAY - 1929
GEORGE GROSZ

After observing the horrors of war as a soldier in WWI, Grosz focused his art on the economic chasm created by the war. He became deeply involved with left wing pacifist activity, publishing drawings in critical and satirical periodicals and participating in protests.

His drawings and paintings from the Weimar era sharply criticized what Grosz viewed as the decay of society. Shortly before Hitler seized power, Grosz moved to America to teach art, thus avoiding persecution by the Nazis who deemed his work "degenerate".

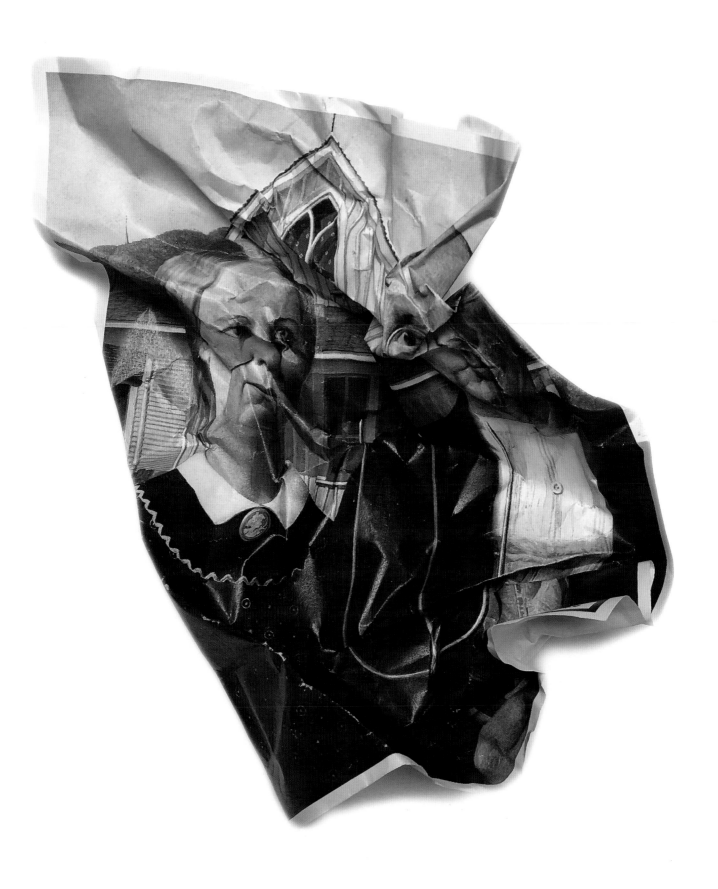

American Gothic - 1930
Grant Wood

Grant Wood decided to paint the kind of people he fancied should live in that house. He recruited his sister Nan to model the woman, dressing her in a colonial print apron mimicking 19th-century Americana. The man is modeled on Wood's former dentist, Dr. Byron McKee from Cedar Rapids, Iowa. Nan, perhaps embarrassed about being depicted as the wife of a man twice her age, told people that her brother had envisioned the couple as father and daughter, rather than husband and wife, which Wood himself confirmed. Therefore, the prim lady with him is his daughter.

COMPOSITION II IN RED, BLUE, AND YELLOW - 1930
PIET MONDRIAN

Piet Mondrian was a Dutch artist, who is regarded as one of the greatest artists of the 20th century, known for being one of the pioneers of abstract art. He changed his direction from figurative painting to an increasingly abstract style, reaching a point where his art grammar was reduced to simple geometric elements.

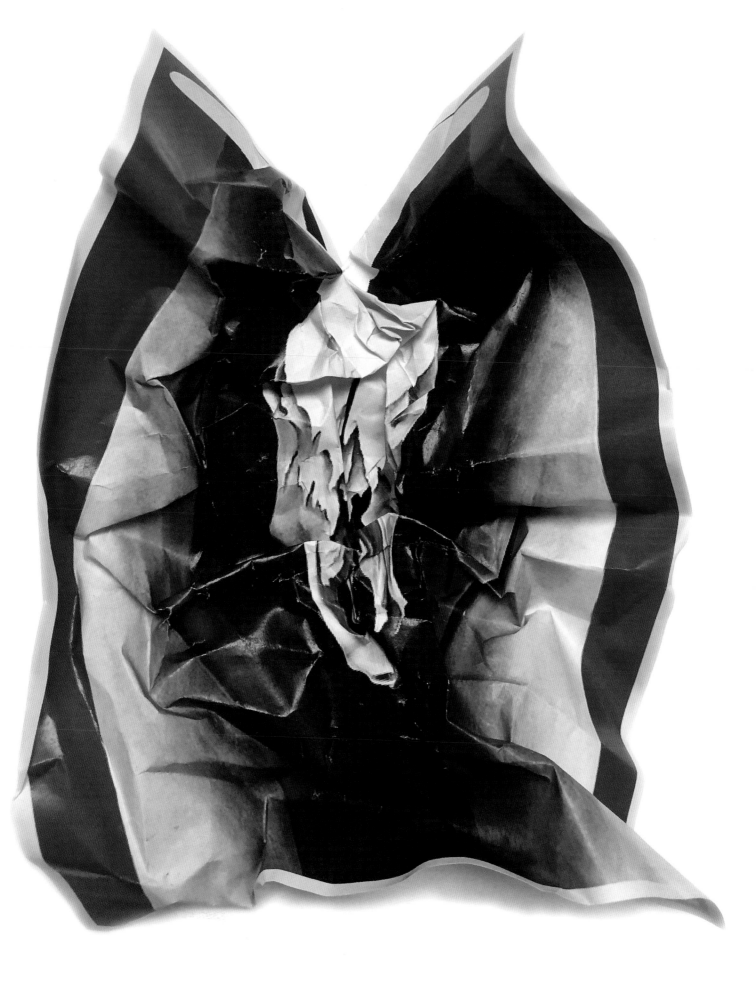

COW'S SKULL: RED, WHITE, & BLUE - 1931
GEORGIA O'KEEFFE

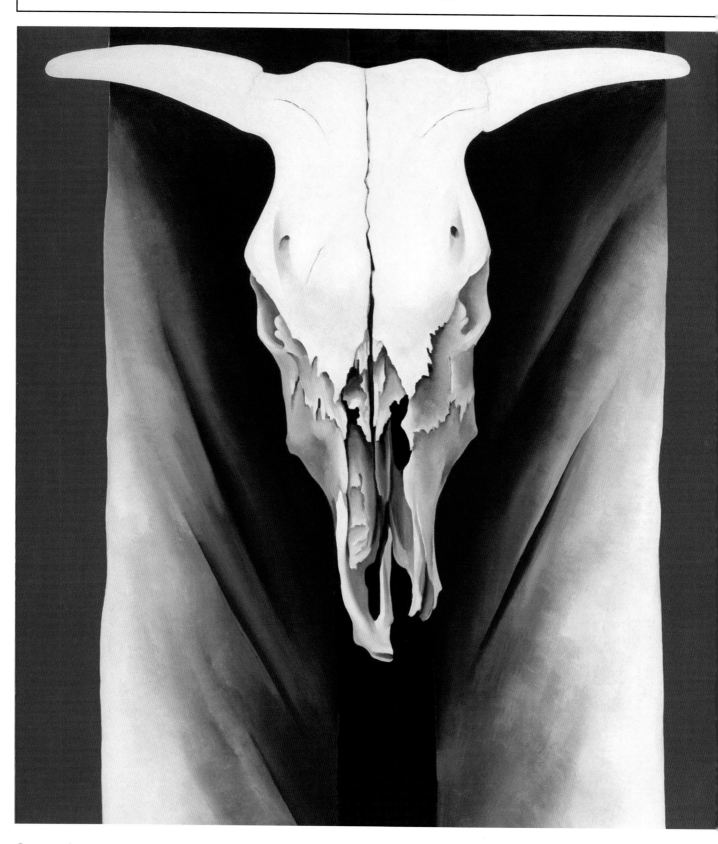

Georgia O'Keeffe used a weathered cow's skull to represent the enduring spirit of America. The painting prominently displays the three colours of the American flag behind the skull. Although she said she made it as a joke on the concept of the "Great American Painting," the picture has become quintessential icon of the American West.

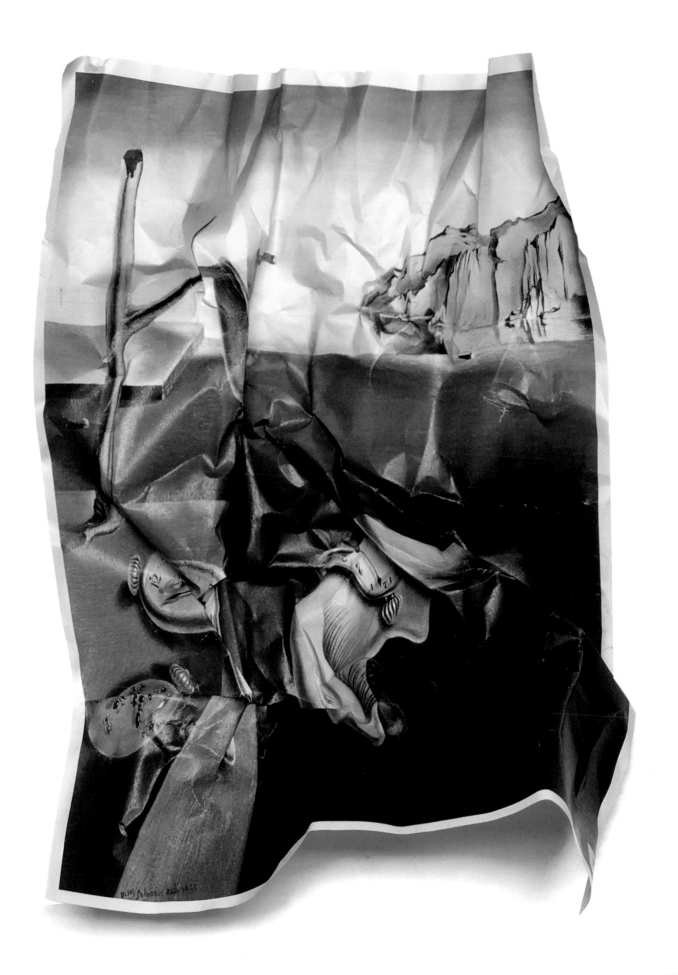

THE PERSISTENCE OF MEMORY - 1931
SALVADOR DALI

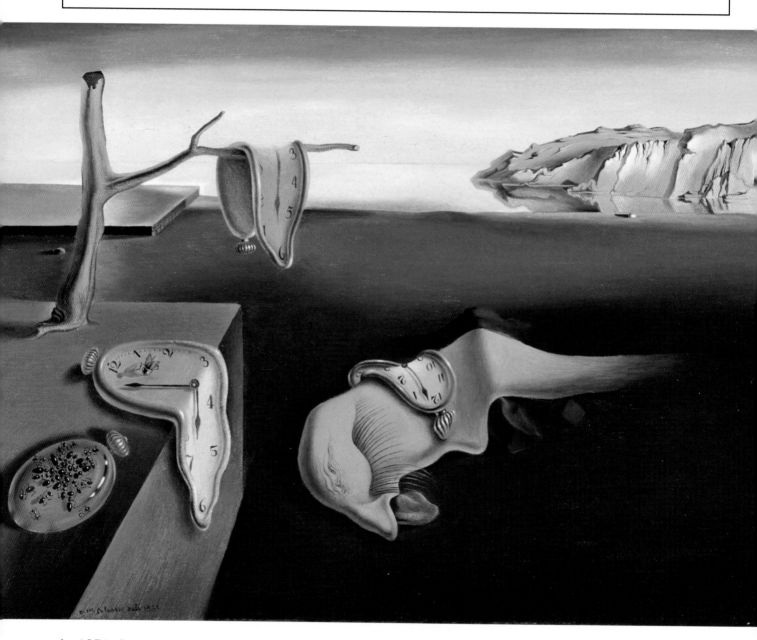

In 1931, Dali perfected his "paranoiac-critical method". The artist would enter into a meditative psychotic state. "I am the first to be surprised and often terrified by the images I see appear upon my canvas." (The Persistence of Memory is one of Dalì's biggest triumphs, but the actual oil-on-canvas painting measures only 9.5 inches by 13 inches.)

TRANSIENTS - 1932
RAPHAEL SOYER

Raphael Soyer in his paintings, drawings, watercolours, and prints, persistently investigated a number of themes—female nudes, portraits of friends and family, New York and, especially, its people. He also painted a vast number of self-portraits and was adamant in his belief in representational art, and during the late 1940s and early 1950s strongly opposed the dominant force of abstract art. Defending his position, he stated: "I choose to be a realist and a humanist in art." He was an artist of the Great Depression, and during the 1930s, Raphael and his twin brother Moses engaged in Social Realism, demonstrating empathy with the struggles of the working class.

RESTING DANCER ON HIGH STOOL - 1950
MOSES SOYER

In 1899 Moses Soyer and his twin brother, Raphael, were born in Russia, each considered to be one of the most important figurative artists of the twentieth century. In 1912, their father, a Hebrew scholar, writer and teacher emigrated to the United States. Influenced by Bonnard and Degas, Soyer is known for his portraits of everyday people, ballerinas and nudes. His works very often depict intimate moments of his subjects in quiet reflection. He died in the Chelsea Hotel in New York while painting dancer and choreographer Phoebe Neville.

CARGADOR DE FLORES - 1935
DIEGO RIVERA

In the summer of 1911, Diego completed an academic art course at the prestigious Mexican Art Academy of San Carlos. In search of his raison d'etre, Rivera, feeling that his training did not help him discover why he was an artist, left for Paris. He thought that art should be enjoyed by everyone especially poor, working people. For ten years he would argue, study and paint, but still felt that something was absent from his work. His paintings seemed only to be enjoyed by well-educated people who could afford to buy them. This led

him to his interest in politics and deepened his understanding of his native land's ancient masterpieces. Upon returning to Mexico in 1921, he became one of a number of Mexican and foreign artists who received commissions for murals in public buildings which brought to full development his style and his epic approach on subjects that promoted revolutionary ideas. Diego Rivera is remembered and celebrated for his humanistic understanding of the role of the artist and the role of art in society which continues to captivate today's viewers.

OBSERVATORY TIME - THE LOVERS - 1936
MAN RAY

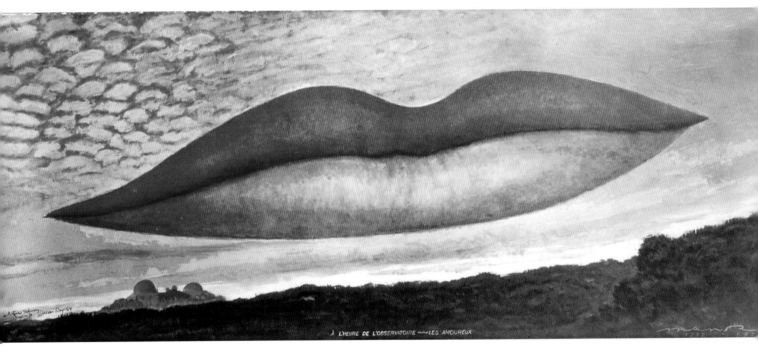

À L'HEURE DE L'OBSERVATOIRE ~ LES AMOUREUX

Observatory Time - The Lovers is one of Man Ray's most recognized and remembered works. The canvas is stretched to a whopping 8 feet by 3 feet. Pictured in the sky hovering over a silhouetted landscape are the lips of his lover, Lee Miller. Miller is said to have influenced Man Ray greatly and her presence is traced throughout much of his art.

GUERNICA - 1937
PABLO PICASSO

In 1937, the Spanish Republican government commissioned Pablo Picasso to create a large piece to exhibit at the Paris World's Fair. Picasso was at a loss as to what he should paint. His initial sketches depicted a painter in his studio, facing a nude model who reclines on a sofa. It was tragedy that led him to change course. Picasso opened his morning paper in Paris on April 27th to find devastating images of the destruction of Guernica. Franco ordered the Nazi Condor Legion (loaned to Franco by Germany) to drop bombs over the small town of Guernica. It was a market day; civilians, predominantly women and children, were convened outdoors in public squares. As the first place where democracy was established in Spain's Basque region, the town was a symbolic target. Picasso began work on a mural about the attack, creating dozens of sketches and plans, eventually producing his 26-foot long, 11-foot wide, black-and-white masterpiece in less than a month and a half. Guernica became the centerpiece of the Spanish pavilion and a sensation at the Fair. Years later, during the Nazi occupation of Paris, on viewing Guernica in Picasso's studio, a Nazi officer asked Picasso," Did you make this painting?" "No," Picasso answered,"YOU did!"

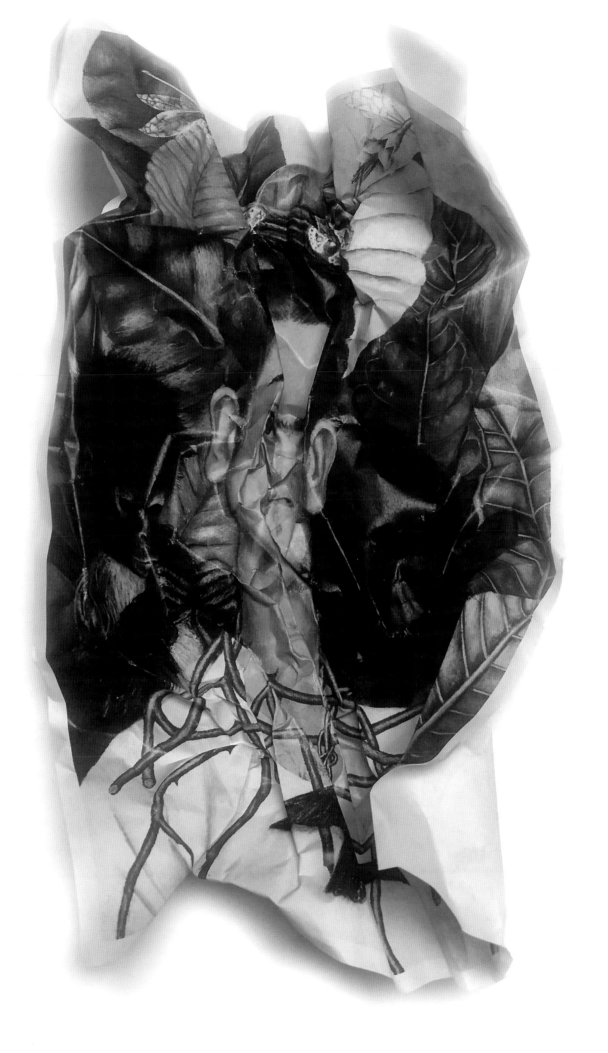

SELF-PORTRAIT-1940
FRIDA KAHLO

Frida Kahlo put many creatures in this painting. She was not painting a realistic scene, but using these symbolic elements to express her feelings. A bird often symbolizes freedom and life, especially a hummingbird, which is colourful and always hovering above flowers. However, in this painting the humming bird is black and lifeless, which is likely a symbol of Frida herself, having spent most of her life in physical pain after being involved in a bus accident when she was eighteen and enduring thirty-five operations. She spent many years bedridden and unable to bear children. Kahlo's painting proved to be eerily prescient when she remarried Diego Rivera in December of 1940. The couple's marital troubles continued. Of their love, Kahlo once said, "I have suffered two grave accidents in my life, one in which a streetcar knocked me down... and the other accident is Diego."

DORA MAAR AU CHAT - 1941
PABLO PICASSO

Dora Maar au Chat is one of Picasso's most valued depictions of his lover and artistic companion. Picasso fell in love at the age of 55 with the 29-year-old Maar and the couple soon began living together. The painting brought the second-highest price ever received at an auction, with the final bid of $95,216,000. Their partnership had been one of intellectual exchange and intense passion—Dora was an artist, spoke Picasso's native Spanish, and shared his political views. She even assisted with the execution of the monumental Guernica and produced the only photo-documentary of the work in progress. She was an intellectual force, a characteristic that both stimulated and challenged Picasso. Her influence spurred him to create the most powerful and daring works of his 75-year career.

NIGHTHAWKS - 1942
EDWARD HOPPER

Nighthawks Edward Hopper's realist painting gives the viewer a look inside 1940s American urban culture. The corner diner is based on a Greenwich Village restaurant. The harsh florescent indoor lighting had just become popular, and lit up the normally very dark street attracting night owls and insomniacs creating a new late-night scene in the village.

THE SON OF MAN - 1946
RENE MAGRITTE

The Son of Man, Magritte said,"shows that everything we see in life hides another thing, and we always want to see what is hidden." In this self-portrait he uses a large, unripened green apple to hide his face.

CHRISTINA'S WORLD - 1948
ANDREW WYETH

With incredible detail, Wyeth depicts his neighbor, Anna Christina Olson, and her family's rural home. Wyeth explained that Olson was physically limited by polio, but by no means spiritually. "The challenge to me," Wyeth said, "was to do justice to her extraordinary conquest of a life which most people would consider hopeless." This painting is housed in New York's Metropolitan Museum of Art's permanent collection.

Autumn Rhythm (No.30) - 1950
Jackson Pollock

Jackson Pollock, one of our most renowned artists, was the master of abstract art who succeeded in realizing a completely new, seemingly simple technique of art-making – 'dripping'. The way he handled paint gave results which merged painting and post-performance products. Pollock felt that the painting itself doesn't mean much without the process behind it. Pollock used to drip and pour paint all over the large canvas which lay on the floor. Moving to the beat of his own inner rhythm, he occasionally used towels and sticks to help him complete the painting. Pollock once said: "Painting is a state of being and self-discovery. Every good artist paints what he is."

THE RUNAWAY - 1958
NORMAN ROCKWELL

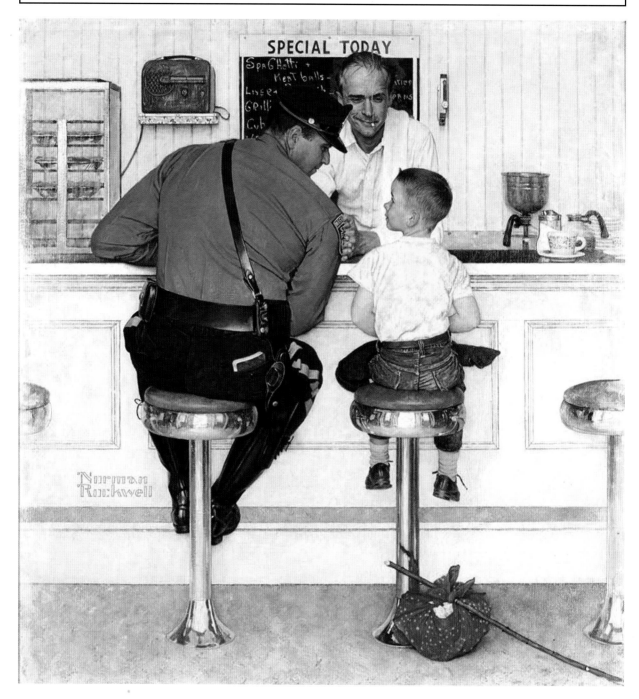

Rockwell once said, "I like to paint kids and I like taking people back in time to their own youth." The Runaway was inspired by Rockwell's firsthand experience stating, "I ran away from home when I was a kid in Mamaroneck and mooned around the shore; kicking stones and watching the whitecaps on Long Island Sound. When it began to get dark and a cold wind sprang up, I went home."

THREE FLAGS - 1958
JASPER JOHNS

This piece is considered one of the most famous artworks of the 20th century. Three American flags are sealed to each other, painted with warm wax, and each is 25% smaller than the previous one. Three Flags is, therefore, not really what you would call a regular painting, but a sculpture consisting of three paintings, descending in size. The piece examines the way abstraction overlaps with representation. The American flag carries a great emblematic connotation, but in the end, it is only stripes and star-shapes. Jasper Johns deliberately goes beyond the limits of a flag, playing with symbols that "the mind already knows," which is an approach typical for Pop Art.

In 1980 the Whitney Museum acquired "The Three Flags" for one million dollars.

TARGET · 1961

JASPER JOHNS

For Target Johns chose a palette of primary colours, a pre-existing schema as found in the image itself. The artist's use of oil and encaustic (pigment mixed with hot wax) created a quick-drying medium that recorded each drag and drip of the brush in almost sculptural terms. These gestural nods to his Abstract predecessors allowed him to investigate the subtle nuances between form and material. There also exists a tension between the idea of the representational (a target) and the notion of the abstract (the geometry of concentric circles).

ORANGE, RED, YELLOW - 1961
MARK ROTHKO

The rectangles within this painting do not extend to the edges of the canvas and appear to hover just over its surface. Staring at each coloured segment individually affects the perception of those adjacent to it. The red-orange has a bit of green. The yellow above seems to tint the orange with blue. Forty-two years after his death, Marc Rothko set a record at a Christie's auction, shattered all records for post-war and contemporary art by fetching $87 million.

CAMPBELL'S SOUP CANS (SERIES) - 1962
ANDY WARHOL

In 1962, Andy Warhol stunned the art world with his representation of Campbell's Soup Cans. Using synthetic polymer paint on 32 canvases (each canvas 20" x 16"), he painted all 32 varieties of Campbell's Soup offered at the time. The individual paintings were produced by a print making method—the semi-mechanized screen printing process, using a non-painterly style. Warhol's Campbell's Soup Cans' reliance on themes from popular culture helped to usher in pop art as a major art movement in the United States.

TORN LABEL CAMBELL'S SOUP CANS - 1962
ANDY WARHOL

*Just learned that I was not the first scruncher. In 1962 Andy
Warhol had scrunched the labels on the Campbell's Soup cans.

WHAAM! -1963
ROY LICHTENSTEIN

The work's composition is taken from a panel drawn by Irv Novick which appeared in issue number 89 of All-American Men of War, published by DC Comics in February 1962. From the original panel, Lichtenstein produced preliminary drawings, one of which is in Tate's collection. In this drawing, he set out his first visualisation of the painting, including marking the divide of the original single panel into two parts, confining the main plane to one and the explosion to the other. Revealing Lichtenstein's process of making minor changes during a work's creation, the colour annotations on the drawing differ from the final colours used in the painting, notably the use of yellow instead of white for the letters of 'WHAAM!' To make the final painting, Lichtenstein projected the preparatory study onto the two pre-primed canvases and drew around the projection in pencil before applying the Ben-Day dots. This involved using a homemade aluminium mesh and pushing oil paint through the holes with a small scrubbing brush. On to this, he painted the thick outlines of shapes and areas of solid colour in Magna acrylic resin paint. This use of different materials has made cleaning the painting a particular challenge for conservators.

LIZ 7 - 1963

ANDY WARHOL

In 1963, Warhol first painted this portrait when Elizabeth Taylor was at the height of her career. This highlights Warhol's fascination with celebrity and death. It began in 1962 with his painting of Marilyn Monroe following her suicide. This fascination continued throughout his career. In this portrait Warhol used a publicity photograph for Taylor's film 'Butterfly 8' as the basis for the screenprint. It is typical of his 1960's Pop style with vibrant, flat blocks of colour. This portrait was made for an exhibition at the Tate held in 1965, the same year Warhol famously announced that he was 'retiring' from painting.

BUFFALO II -1964
ROBERT RAUSCHENBERG

On March 1st, 2019, Alice Walton, the billionaire heir to the Walmart fortune, purchased Buffalo II for $88.8 million. The sale represents a major windfall for the heirs of the painting's previous owners, Robert and Beatrice Mayer, who bought Buffalo II (1964) from dealer Leo Castelli for $16,900 (about $140,000 in today's dollars)—a potential return of about 300,000%.

193

A Bigger Splash - 1967
DAVID HOCKNEY

In 1963, a year after graduating from the Royal College of Art, London, David Hockney first visited Los Angeles. He was drawn to California by the relaxed and sensual way of life. Hockney remarked that everybody had a swimming pool. They could be used all year round and were not considered a luxury, unlike in Britain where it is too cold for most of the year. Between 1964 and 1971 he made numerous paintings of California swimming pools, and in 1976 he set up permanent residence there.

This painting recently sold for $4,000,000 and is now on display at the Tate.

TELEPHONE BOOTHS - 1968
RICHARD ESTES

Richard Estes is held to be one of the foremost practitioners of American Photorealism, famed for his meticulous attention to detail and invisible brushwork. Most of his paintings portray urban landscapes and specific details of life in big cities, particularly New York. His most noted work is Telephone Booths. Although the scene depicted is recognizable, the complexity of the optical angle and the jumble of reflections requires an additional effort of concentration, as nothing can be registered at first sight. As in most of his paintings, Estes explores the ability of glass to mislead, as it can both be transparent and reflect at the same time, a fact which further heightens its bewildering effect.

MAY 1968 - 1973
JOAN MIRO

The painting's title, May 1968, refers to the date when France was marked by student protests against capitalism, consumerism and traditional institutions. 22% of the nation's population were involved in these strikes. Many have considered this a cultural, social and moral turning point in the history of the country. Joan Miro, who sympathized with the movement, was inspired by its events to create this work of art capturing the spirit of the rebellion.

FIRE OF DATTAN - 1976
KAZUO SHIRAGA

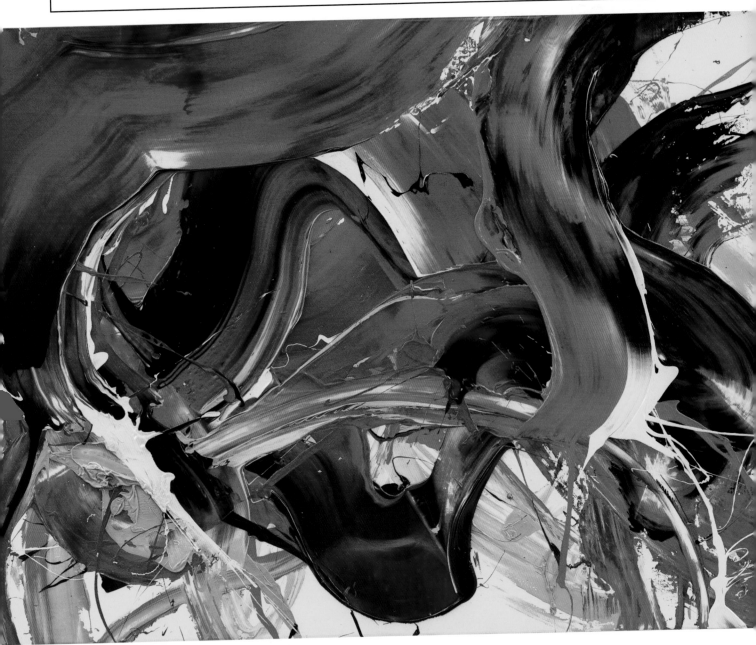

Kazuo Shiraga (August 12, 1924 – April 8, 2008) was a modern artist who was a member of the Gutai group of avant-garde artists. Shiraga developed as an artist during his six-decade career honing his singular technique of painting suspended from a rope, using his feet to make violently abstract, thickly impasted canvases. It has only been since the artist's death, however, that the conceptual originality and visual power of these "foot paintings" have been recognized by Western curators and collectors. Then, in 1971, he adopted the Buddist philosophy and became a monk. The title of this work, which is often times referred to as Fire of Dattan, refers to the Buddhist ritual where monks dance and wield a large torch of burning fire as an act of renewal. Such a motif aptly matches the artist's refreshed psychology in the early seventies, and would remain as one of the most important motifs in Shiraga's artistic career.

MARILYN (VANITAS) - 1977
AUDREY FLACK

In this photorealistic still life, Marilyn Monroe is remembered in what could be a shop-window memorial. Flack took her inspiration from the 17th century Vanitas tradition, where the still life is composed of objects that relate to the fleeting 'vanities' of life. Red lipstick, powder, perfume and jewelery can be read, on the one hand, as emblems of Marilyn's public persona, but they act also as universal symbols that speak of the superficial and fragile nature of vanity. Flack's Vanitas are brought into the 20th century through the introduction of modern day objects and photographic imagery, producing what she termed "narrative still lifes". The use of the airbrush to produce rich, sparkling veneers was very unique and thus career defining and securing Flack her rightful place amongst the leading Photorealists of the 1970s.

MARK-1978
CHUCK CLOSE

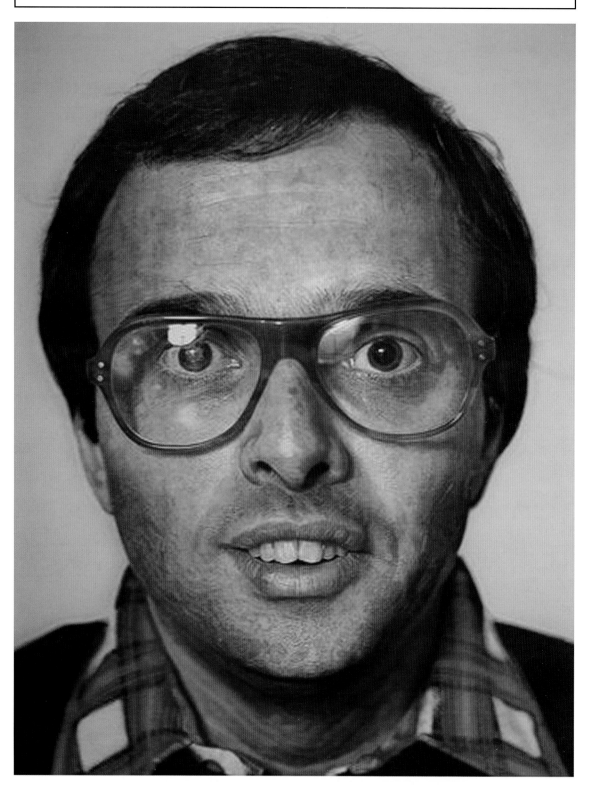

Chuck Close reinvented painting with his monumental portraits, rendered with exacting realism from photographic sources. Playing with ideas of scale, colour, and form, Close became famous for his rigorous, gridded application of individual colour squares, which, although abstract up close, form unified, highly realistic images from afar.

He said,"I think most paintings are a record of the decisions that the artist made. I perhaps make them a little clearer than other's have." Close's artificially restrictive painting techniques stem in part from physical limitations—he suffers from an inability to recognize faces, and had a spinal injury in 1988 that left him largely paralyzed.

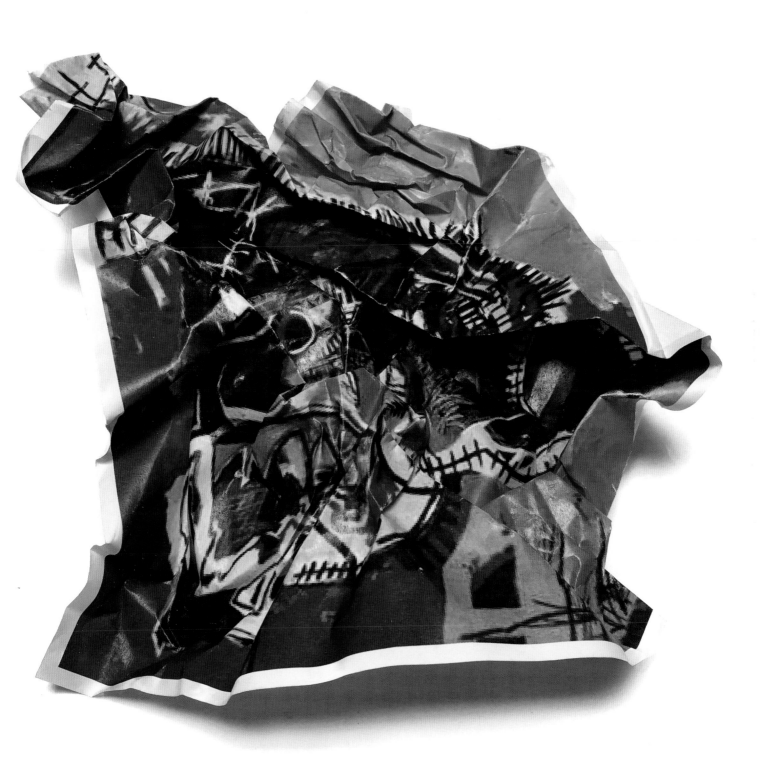

SKULL-1982

JEAN-MICHEL BASQUIAT

Basquiat used social commentary in his paintings as a tool for introspection and for identifying with his experiences in the black community of his time, as well as attacks on power structures and systems of racism. Basquiat's visual poetics were acutely political and direct in their criticism of colonialism and support for class struggle. He died of a heroin overdose at his studio at the age of 27. On May 18, 2017, at a Sotheby's auction, a 1982 painting by Basquiat depicting a black skull with red and black rivulets set a new record high for any American artist at auction, selling for $110.5 million. Basquiat's art has inspired many in the hip hop music community such as Jay-Z.

CRACK IS WACK - 1986
KEITH HARING

Depicting the artist's unique rendering of social and political issues such as sexuality and war, Haring's work stands at the intersection of graffiti and pop art. One of Haring's most famous works is a mural he painted in 1986 on a handball court at 128th Street and 2nd Ave. in Harlem.

Crack is Wack was a direct response to the crack epidemic that swept New York City in the 1980s. The mural was never commissioned, nor did the city grant Haring permission to paint it, but Haring executed the piece as a personal warning. The mural still exists today, protected by the City.

Haring died on February 16, 1990, of AIDS-related complications. He was only 31.

ABALONE ACETONE POWDER - 1991
DAMIEN HIRST

Gallery visitor viewing Damien Hirst's "Spots"

Hirst explains that, "With my spot paintings, I probably discovered that the most fundamentally important thing in any kind of art is the harmony of where colour can exist on its own, interacting with other colours in a perfect format." Any problems Hirst previously had with colour were removed by the perfect arrangement of complimentary, yet never repeated, colours in the spots.

BUTTERFLY SPIN PAINTING - 2009
DAMIEN HIRST

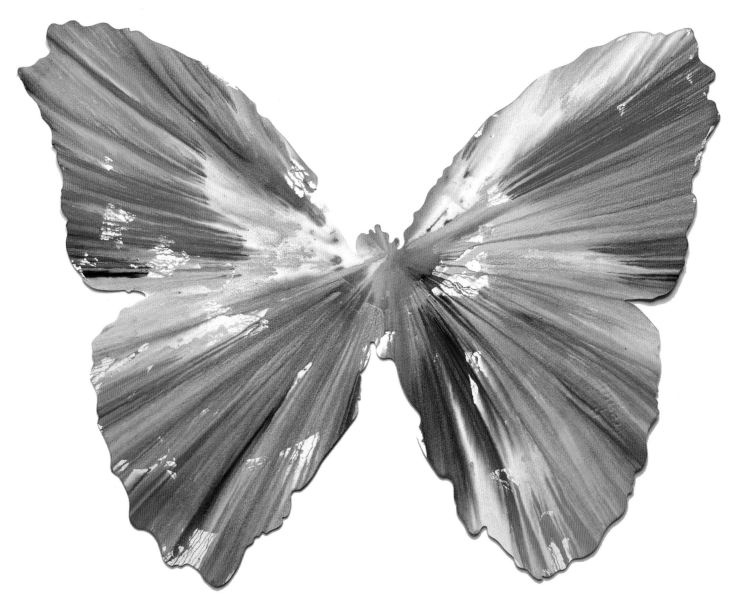

Damien Hirst describes his "Spin" paintings, the psychedelic compositions that harken back to his youth in the 1960s, as "childish...in the positive sense of the word." By the 1990s, "spin paintings" formed an integral part of his work. Hirst had his 'spin machine' in his Berlin studio, allowing him to further play with the process. Since then, his spinning works have become as iconic as his meticulous "spot paintings".

SNOW - 2018
BANKSY

Locals in the Welsh town of Port Talbot—the most polluted area in the UK, and one of the nation's "most deprived," according to the BBC—woke up to an early Christmas present one Wednesday morning: a new painting by Banksy. Port Talbot is home to the largest steel plant in the UK. Blackdust, the plant's byproduct, covered the town. As a layer of soot settled on streets, cars, and playgrounds, locals complained of major respiratory issues.

fini

OTHER WORKS BY CARL REINER:

"Enter Laughing"

"The 2000 Year Old Man:
The Complete History"

"All Kinds of Love"

"Continue Laughing"

"The 2000 Year Old Man in
the Year 2000: The Book"

"How Paul Robeson Saved My Life
And Other Mostly Happy Stories"

"My Anecdotal Life"

"NNNNN"

"Just Desserts: A Novellelah"

"I Remember Me"

"I Just Remembered"

"What I Forgot To Remember"

"Why and When The Dick Van Dyke Show Was Born"

"Carl Reiner, Now You're Ninety-Four"

"Too Busy To Die"

"How To Live Forever"

"Alive at Ninety-Five
Recalling Movies I Love"
(1928-1950)

"Approaching Ninety-Six
The Films I love Viewing & Loved Doing"
(1951-1917)

"The Downing of Trump"

"I Remember Radio"

"Scrunched Photos of Celebrities"

CHILDREN'S BOOKS:

"Tell Me A Scary Story
But Not Too Scary!"

"The 2000 Year Old Man
Goes To School"

"Tell Me Another Scary Story
But Not Too Scary!"

"Tell Me A Silly Story"

"Too Scared To Scream"

"The Secret Treasure Of Tahka Paka"

"You Say God Bless You For Sneezing & Farting"

BROADWAY PLAYS:

"Something Different"

"Shakespeare Was Wrong"
The Play Is Not The Thing The Audience Is"